Love

in praise and celebration

SELECTED FOR HALLMARK BY HELEN EXLEY

Hallmark
GIFT BOOKS

BOK 4038

EXLEY

... the world was newly crowned
With flowers, when
first we met.

THOMAS HOOD (1799-1845), FROM "THE TIME OF ROSES"

There is nothing holier, in this life of ours, than the first
consciousness of love – the first fluttering of its silken wings.

HENRY WADSWORTH LONGFELLOW (1807-1882)

Every kiss provokes another. Ah, in those earliest days of
love how naturally the kisses spring into life. How closely,
in their abundance, are they pressed one against another;
until lovers would find it as hard to count the kisses
exchanged in an hour, as to count the flowers
in a meadow in May.

MARCEL PROUST (1871-1922), FROM "SWANN'S WAY"

A sunbeam filtering through the blind shed a gentle light on her soft golden hair, on her pure throat, on her tranquil breast.... It seemed to me that I had known her for a long time, and that before her I had known nothing and had not lived.... "And here I am sitting opposite her," I was thinking, "I have met her; I know her. God, what happiness!" I almost leapt from my chair in ecstasy....

IVAN TURGENEV, FROM "FIRST LOVE"

I think the time has come, it really has come for us to do a little courting. Have we ever had time to stand under trees and tell our love? Or to sit down by the sea and make fragrant zones for each other? Do you know the peculiar exquisite scent of a tea-rose?

Do you know how the bud opens – so unlike other roses and how deep red the thorns are and almost purple the leaves?

Wander with me 10 years – will you, darling? Ten years in the sun. It's not long – only 10 springs.

Katherine Mansfield (1888-1923),
from "Letters to John Middleton Murry"

When two souls, which have sought each other for however long in the throng, have finally found each other, when they have seen that they are matched, are in sympathy and compatible, in a word, that they are alike, there is then established for ever between them a union, fiery and pure as they themselves are, a union which begins on earth and continues for ever in heaven. This union is love, true love, such as in truth very few men can conceive of, that love which is a religion, which deifies the loved one, whose life comes from devotion and passion, and for which the greatest sacrifices are the sweetest delights.

VICTOR HUGO (1802-1885), TO ADÈLE FOUCHER

Love isn't decent. Love is glorious and shameless.

ELIZABETH VON ARNIM (1866-1941), FROM "LOVE"

Submit to love faithfully and it gives a person joy. It intoxicates, it envelops, it isolates. It creates fragrance in the air, ardour from coldness, it beautifies everything around it.

LEOŠ JANÁČEK (1854-1928), TO KAMILA STÖSSLOVÁ

The madness of love is the greatest of heaven's blessings.

PLATO (427-347 B.C.), FROM "PHAEDRUS"

To love is the great Amulet that makes this world a garden.

ROBERT LOUIS STEVENSON (1850-1894)

Love always creates, it never destroys. In this lies man's only promise.

LEO BUSCAGLIA, FROM "LOVE"

Yes, it was beginning in each

Yes, it threw waves across our lives

Yes, the pulses were becoming very strong

Yes, the beating became very delicate

Yes, the calling   the arousal

Yes, the arriving   the coming

Yes, there it was for both entire

Yes, we were looking at each other

MURIEL RUKEYSER (1913-1980),
FROM "LOOKING AT EACH OTHER"

Now we will feel no rain

for each of us will be shelter for the other.

Now we will feel no cold

for each of us will be warmth for the other.

Now there is no more loneliness

for each of us will be companion to the other.

There is only one life before us

and our seasons will be long and good.

ADAPTED FROM THE APACHE

[Love is] something like the clouds that were in the sky before the sun came out. You cannot touch the clouds, you know; but you feel the rain and know how glad the flowers and the thirsty earth are to have it after a hot day. You cannot touch love either; but you feel the sweetness that it pours into everything.

ANNIE SULLIVAN (1866-1936)

THE HEART'S FRIEND

Fair is the white star of twilight,
And the sky clearer
At the day's end;
   But she is fairer, and she is dearer,
   She, my heart's friend!

Fair is the white star of twilight,
And the moon roving
To the sky's end;
   But she is fairer, better worth loving,
   She, my heart's friend.

SHOSHONE LOVE SONG

The actual thing – inloveness – requires something like a spark leaping back and forth from one to the other becoming more intense every moment, love building up like voltage in a coil. Here there is no sound of one hand clapping…. One who has never been in love might mistake either infatuation or a mixture of affection and sexual attraction for being in love. But when the "real thing" happens, there is no doubt. A man in the jungle at night, as someone said, may suppose a hyena's growl to be a lion's; but when he hears the lion's growl, he knows damn' well it's a lion. So with the genuine inloveness.

SHELDON VANAUKEN

Who,
being loved,
is poor?

OSCAR WILDE (1856-1900)

I met in the street

a very poor young man

who was in love.

His hat was old,

his coat worn,

his cloak

was out at the elbows,

the water passed

through his shoes, –

and the stars through

his soul.

VICTOR HUGO (1802-1885)

your slightest look easily will

    unclose me

though i have closed myself as

    fingers,

you open always petal by petal

    myself as Spring opens

(touching skilfully,mysteriously)her

    first rose

E.E. CUMMINGS (1864-1962),
FROM "SOMEWHERE I HAVE NEVER
TRAVELLED, GLADLY BEYOND"

... IN A POOR MOUNTAIN HUT

Gladly I'll live in a poor mountain hut,

Spin, sew, and till the soil in any weather,

And wash in the cold mountain stream, if but

We dwell together.

ANONYMOUS

Peace flows into me

　　　　As the tide to the pool by the shore;

　　　　It is mine forevermore,

It will not ebb like the sea.

I am the pool of blue

　　　　That worships the vivid sky;

　　　　My hopes were heaven-high,

They are all fulfilled in you.

I am the pool of gold

　　　　When sunset burns and dies –

　　　　You are my deepening skies;

Give me your stars to hold.

SARA TEASDALE (1884-1933)

He carried her to the window, so that she too, saw the view. They sank upon their knees, invisible from the road, they hoped, and began to whisper one another's names. Ah! it was worth while; it was the great joy that they had expected, and countless little joys of which they had never dreamt....

Then they spoke of other things – the desultory talk of those who have been fighting to reach one another, and whose reward is to rest quietly in each other's arms.

E.M. FORSTER (1879-1970), FROM "A ROOM WITH A VIEW"

. . .Give all to love;
Obey thy heart;
Friends, kindred, days,
Estate, good fame,
Plans, credit and the Muse –
Nothing refuse.

'Tis a brave master;
Let it have scope;
Follow it utterly,
Hope beyond hope:

High and more high
It dives into noon,
With wing unspent,
Untold intent;
But it is a god,
Knows its own path,
And the outlets of the sky....

RALPH WALDO EMERSON (1803-1882)

*Who travels for love finds a thousand miles
not longer than one.*

JAPANESE PROVERB

Love feels no burden, thinks nothing of trouble, attempts what is above its strength, pleads no excuse of impossibility.... It is therefore able to undertake all things, and it completes many things, and warrants them to take effect, where he who does not love would faint and lie down. Love is watchful and sleeping, slumbereth not. Though weary, it is not tired; though pressed, it is not straitened; though alarmed, it is not confounded; but, as a lively flame and burning torch, it forces its way upwards and securely passes all.

THOMAS À KEMPIS (1379-1471)

It is the true season of Love when we know that we alone can love, that no one could ever have loved before us and that no one will ever Love in the same way after us.

JOHANN WOLFGANG VON GOETHE (1749-1832)

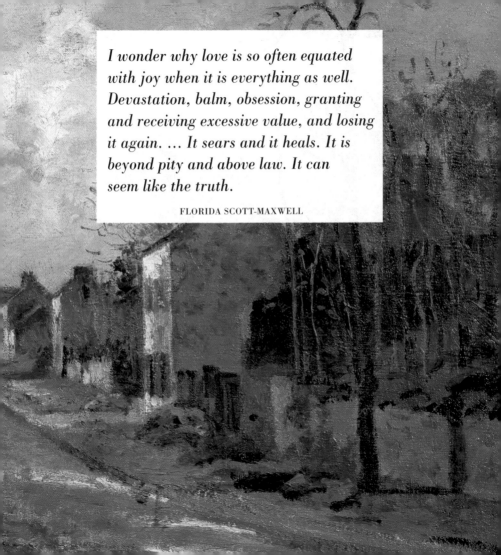

I wonder why love is so often equated with joy when it is everything as well. Devastation, balm, obsession, granting and receiving excessive value, and losing it again. … It sears and it heals. It is beyond pity and above law. It can seem like the truth.

FLORIDA SCOTT-MAXWELL

"I mean that I love you," he said quietly. "You can keep the knowledge, if you care to and it means anything to you. I didn't intend to tell you, but I am told that women like the thought of hopeless love; the more the merrier, perhaps. A little trophy for you, something to hang on your bracelet – like this!" He took off his signet-ring, kissed it and put it into her hand. "When you are an old lady, you can show it to your grandchildren, and say, 'That one was Esmé's – or was it Tom's, or Dick's or Harry's?'"

... She put one palm over the other, the ring safe between them, and wondered what to say. She wanted to clutch at some of his words before they faded, but already they were flying away from her.... "I haven't thanked you. For the ring, I mean, and for what you said.

"No words will come. All I can say is that I love you, too, and have for years and shall for ever."

ELIZABETH TAYLOR (1912-1975), FROM "ANGEL"

PLUCKING THE RUSHES

Green rushes with red shoots,
Long leaves bending to the wind –
You and I in the same boat
Plucking rushes at the Five Lakes.
We started at dawn from the orchid-island:
We rested under the elms till noon.
You and I plucking rushes
Had not plucked a handful when night came!

ANONYMOUS
Translated from the Chinese by Arthur Waley

When love beckons to you, follow him,
Though his ways are hard and steep.
And when his wings enfold you yield to him,
Though the sword hidden among his pinions
*   may wound you.*
And when he speaks to you believe in him,

Though his voice may shatter your dreams as
the north wind lays waste the garden.

For even as love crowns you so shall he crucify
you. Even as he is for your growth so is he for
your pruning....

... if in your fear you would seek only love's
peace and love's pleasure,
Then it is better for you that you cover your
nakedness and pass out of love's
threshing-floor,
Into the seasonless world where you shall
laugh, but not all of your laughter, and weep,
but not all of your tears.

KAHLIL GIBRAN (1883-1931), FROM "THE PROPHET"

It seems to me, to myself, that no man was ever before to any woman what you are to me – the fulness must be in proportion, you know, to the vacancy ... and only I know what was behind – the long wilderness without the blossoming rose ... and the capacity for happiness, like a black gaping hole, before this silver flooding. Is it wonderful that I should stand as in a dream, and disbelieve – not you – but my own fate? Was ever anyone taken suddenly from a lampless dungeon and placed upon the pinnacle of a mountain, without the head turning round and the heart turning faint, as mine do?

**ELIZABETH BARRETT (1806-1861),
TO ROBERT BROWNING**

Love vanquishes time. To lovers, a moment can be eternity, eternity can be the tick of a clock. Across the barriers of time and the ultimate destiny, love persists, for the home of the beloved, absent or present, is always in the mind and heart. Absence does not diminish love.

MARY PARRISH, b.1905, FROM "MCCALLS" MAGAZINE

The need to surrender is one of the great paradoxes of love. Surrender may seem like giving up. Or giving in. But in reality we are strengthened when we actively choose to make ourselves vulnerable. We are empowered by sharing our deepest self with another person, offering him or her our heart, our soul, our life. Surrender is an act of free will. A sacred trust.

ELLEN SUE STERN

I am writing to you, my pen dipped in the pine scent of this afternoon, so that you can breathe the words in and find the image I have for you in my heart. The letters swim in the Adriatic turquoise and clear midsummer skies. There are islands between the paragraphs.... Further still await the satin mountains. Feel the caress of their mystical invitation. I am writing to you, while fish leap between the commas and fullstops.... I hold a stone, a warm pulse in my hand that contains the sun. It is time itself, your time, my time. I parcel it to you, inscribed with memories that flow into deeper hues with each breath.

STEPHANIE JUNE SORRELL, b.1956

I want my rapscallionly fellow vagabond.
  I want my dark lady. I want my angel –
I want my tempter. I want
  my Freia with her apples. I want the lighter of
my seven lamps of beauty, honour, laughter,
  music, love, life and immortality ... I want
my inspiration, my folly, my happiness,
  my divinity, my madness, my selfishness,
my final sanity and sanctification,
  my transfiguration, my purification,
my light across the sea,
  my palm across the desert,
my garden of lovely flowers,
  my million nameless joys,
my day's wage,
  my night's dream,
my darling and
  my star....

GEORGE BERNARD SHAW (1856-1950), TO BEATRICE CAMPBELL

… In our life there is a
single color,
as on an artist's palette,
which provides the
meaning of life and art.
It is the color of love.

MARC CHAGALL, FROM "NEWSWEEK", APRIL 8, 1985

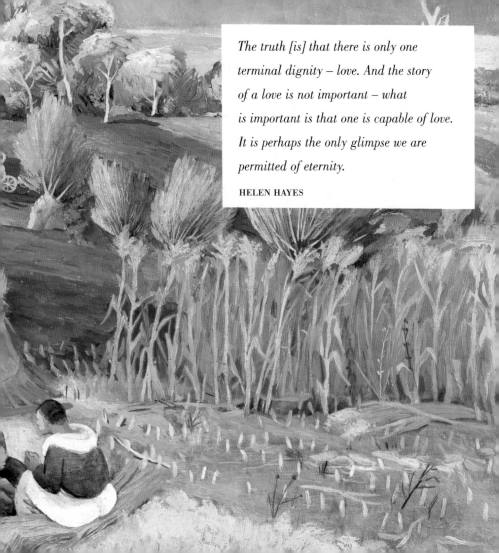

The truth [is] that there is only one terminal dignity – love. And the story of a love is not important – what is important is that one is capable of love. It is perhaps the only glimpse we are permitted of eternity.

HELEN HAYES

... You came, and the sun
came after,
And the green grew golden
above;
And the flag-flowers lightened
with laughter,
And the meadow-sweet
shook with love.

ALGERNON CHARLES SWINBURNE (1837-1909),
FROM "AN INTERLUDE"

Here we are
running with the weeds
colors exaggerated
pistils wild
embarrassing the calm family flowers Oh
here we are
flourishing for the field
and the name of the place
is Love

LUCILLE CLIFTON, b.1936, "FLOWERS"

A life without love in it is like a heap of ashes upon a deserted hearth – with the fire dead, the laughter stilled, and the light extinguished.

FRANK P. TEBBETTS

Of all forms of caution, caution in love is perhaps the most fatal to true happiness.

BERTRAND RUSSELL (1872-1970)

To cheat oneself out of love is the most terrible deception; it is an eternal loss for which there is no reparation, either in time or in eternity.

SÖREN KIERKEGAARD (1813-1855)

Summer Poem

I will bring you flowers
every morning for your breakfast
and you will kiss me
with flowers in your mouth
and you will bring me flowers
every morning when you wake
and look at me with flowers in your eyes

HEATHER HOLDEN

During the fleeting weeks of that single summer, I lived through my first experience of intense love. All the poetry in my nature centred itself with sudden passion upon a single girl. For me she was the sun and moon, the sea, the hills, and the rivers, the cornfields, the hayfields, the plough-lands, and the first stars of nightfall. Everything that is lovely in nature became illumined by the thought of her....

From the moment I had seen her in the church I could think of nothing else. My whole approach to life was altered. I no longer cared whether I was to be a poet or not a poet, I no longer was concerned with the deeper problems of existence. Unless I could associate what I saw, heard, tasted, smelt, and touched with her I no longer give it attention.

What reason was there for me to heed the waves that broke day and night against the irregular coasts of the world, to exult in the grass that grew day and night upon the broad back of the stationary land, to watch from ancient elbow-bone bridges the flowing away of rivers, to look up at the crafty midnight stars, unless such appearances could be made to serve in some way as poetical settings for this girl of my utter idolatry? It seemed to me then, as indeed it seems to me still, that every inch of her body shone with some mysterious light....

LLEWELYN POWYS (1884-1939), FROM "LOVE AND DEATH"

My eyes want to kiss your face.

I have no power over my eyes.

They just want to kiss your face.

I flow towards you out of my eyes,

a fine heat trembles round your shoulders,

it slowly dissolves your contours

and I am there with you, your mouth

and everywhere around you –

I have no power over my eyes.

SOLVEIG VON SCHOULTZ, b.1907, FROM "THE LOVER"

Amid the gloom and travail of existence
suddenly to behold a beautiful being, and
as instantaneously to feel an
overwhelming conviction that with that
fair form for ever our destiny must be
entwined; that there is no more joy than in
her joy, no sorrow but when she grieves;
that in her sigh of love, in her smile of
fondness, hereafter is all bliss; to feel our
flaunty ambition fade away like a
shrivelled gourd before her vision; to feel
fame a juggle and posterity a lie; and to be
prepared at once, for this great object, to
forfeit and fling away all former hopes,
ties, schemes, views; to violate in her
favour every duty of society; this is a lover,
and this is love.

BENJAMIN DISRAELI (1804-1881), FROM "HENRIETTA TEMPLE"

I am writing to you on Sunday evening, which is the time I like to write to you best, because I feel the quietest and descend the most into my real self, where my love is strongest and deepest. So you know I always have a fancy at such times that our love makes us somehow alone together in the world. We seem to have a deep life together apart from all other people on earth, and which we cannot show, explain or impart to them. At least my affection seems to isolate me in the deepest moments from all others, and it makes me speak with my whole heart and soul to you and you only.

WALTER BAGEHOT (1826-1877), TO ELIZA WILSON, 1858

We are the dupes of myth when we upbraid

Ourselves because we love; for we are made

For loving: all the sweets of living are

For those that love. Be joyful, unafraid!

THE RUBAIYAT OF OMAR KHAYYAM

*Perhaps, after all, romance
did not come into one's life with pomp
and blare, like a gay knight riding
down; perhaps it crept to one's side
like an old friend through quiet ways;
perhaps it revealed itself in seeming
prose, until some sudden shaft of
illumination flung athwart its pages
betrayed the rhythm and the music;
perhaps ... perhaps ... love unfolded
naturally out of a beautiful
friendship, as a golden-hearted rose
slipping from its green sheath.*

**L. M. MONTGOMERY (1874-1942),
FROM "ANNE OF AVONLEA"**

These were the days of her poetry, and she said to herself – and she said it too to him, her lips against his ear – that he had made the difference in her life between an unlit room and the same room when a lamp is brought in; a beautiful lamp, she whispered, with a silver stem, and its flame the colour of the heart of a rose.

And Christopher's answer was the answer of all young lovers not two days married, and it did seem to them both that they were actually in heaven.

ELIZABETH VON ARNIM (1866-1941), FROM "LOVE"

... I never see beauty without thinking of you or scent happiness without thinking of you. You have fulfilled all my ambition, realized all my hopes, made all my dreams come true.

You have set a crown of roses on my youth and fortified me against the disaster of our days.

DUFF COOPER (1890-1954)

Lovers don't finally meet somewhere. They're in each other all along.

JALALU'DDIN RUMI, FROM "OPEN SECRET"

Though neither of us was aware of the other before we met, there was a kind of mindless certainty humming along beneath our ignorance that insured we would come together. Like two solitary birds flying the great prairies by celestial reckoning, all of these years and lifetimes we have been moving toward one another.

ROBERT JAMES WALLER, b.1939,
FROM "THE BRIDGES OF MADISON COUNTY"

TO HIS LOVE

Shall I compare thee to a summer's day?
Thou art more lovely and more temperate;
Rough winds do shake the darling buds of May,
And summer's lease hath all too short a date:
Sometimes too hot the eye of heaven shines,
And often is his gold complexion dimm'd;
And every fair from fair some time declines,
By chance, or nature's changing course, untrimm'd.
But thy eternal summer shall not fade
Nor lose possession of that fair thou ow'st,
Nor shall Death brag thou wand'rest in his shade
When in eternal lines to time thou grow'st,
So long as men can breathe, or eyes can see,
So long lives this, and this gives life to thee.

WILLIAM SHAKESPEARE (1564-1616)

To hold her in my arms against the twilight

and be her comrade for ever – this was all I

wanted so long as my life should last.... And

this, I told myself with a kind of wonder, this

was what love was: this consecration, this

curious uplifting, this sudden inexplicable joy,

and this intolerable pain.

A N O N Y M O U S

PICTURE CREDITS

TEXT CREDITS